THIS BOOK BELONGS TO :

....

....

Q)

WHAT HAPPENS IF YOU EAT CHRISTMAS DECORATIONS?

A)

YOU GET TINSELITUS

Q)

WHAT DO YOU CALL SANTA WHEN HE STOPS MOVING?

A)

SANTA PAUSE

Q)

WHY WAS THE LITTLE BOY SO COLD ON CHRISTMAS MORNING?

A)

BECAUSE IT WAS DECEMBRRRRR!

Q)

WHAT COMES AT THE END OF CHRISTMAS DAY?

A)

THE LETTER "Y!"

Q)

WHAT DO SNOWMEN EAT FOR BREAKFAST?

A)

SNOWFLAKES

Q)

WHY DO MUMMIES LIKE CHRISTMAS SO MUCH?

A)

BECAUSE OF ALL THE WRAPPING!

Q)

WHAT HAPPENED TO THE THIEF WHO STOLE A CHRISTMAS CALENDAR?

A)

HE GOT 12 MONTHS.

Q)

WHAT DOES AN ELF STUDY IN SCHOOL?

A)

THE ELFABET.

Q)

WHAT DO YOU GET IF YOU MIX A VAMPIRE WITH A SNOWMAN?

A)

FROSTBITE.

Q)

WHAT'S ANOTHER NAME FOR SANTA'S LITTLE HELPERS?

A)

SUBORDINATE CLAUSES.

Q)

WHAT IS A COW'S FAVORITE HOLIDAY?

A)

MOO-YEARS DAY.

Q)

WHAT DOES SANTA SUFFER FROM WHENEVER HE GETS STUCK IN A CHIMNEY?

A)

SANTA CLAUSTROPHOBIA

Q)

HOW DO SHEEP WISH EACH OTHER HAPPY HOLIDAYS?

A)

MERRY CHRISTMAS TO EWE.

Q)

WHAT IS AN ELF'S FAVORITE SPORT?

A)

NORTH-POLE VAULTING.

Q)

WHAT DOES MRS. CLAUS SAY TO SANTA WHEN THERE ARE CLOUDS IN THE SKY?

A)

IT LOOKS LIKE RAIN, DEER.

Q)

WHAT DO SNOWMEN TAKE WHEN THE SUN GETS TOO HOT?

A)

A CHILL PILL.

Q)

WHAT SHOULD YOU GIVE YOUR PARENTS AT CHRISTMAS?

A)

A LIST OF WHAT YOU WANT.

Q)

WHAT DID THE GINGERBREAD MAN PUT UNDER HIS BLANKETS?

A)

A COOKIE SHEET.

Q)

WHO DELIVERS CHRISTMAS PRESENTS TO ELEPHANTS?

A)

ELEPHANTA CLAUS.

Q)

HOW DOES RUDOLPH KNOW WHEN CHRISTMAS IS COMING?

A)

HE REFERS TO HIS CALEN-DEER.

Q)

WHERE DOES A SNOWMAN KEEP HIS MONEY?

A)

IN A SNOW BANK.

Q)

WHAT DO YOU CALL A GREEDY ELF?

A)

ELFISH!

Q)

HOW DOES RUDOLPH KNOW WHEN CHRISTMAS IS COMING?

A)

HE REFERS TO HIS CALEN-DEER.

Q)

WHY WOULDN'T THE CHRISTMAS TREE STAND UP?

A)

IT HAD NO LEGS.

Q)

WHY DIDN'T RUDOLPH GET A GOOD REPORT CARD?

A)

BECAUSE HE WENT DOWN IN HISTORY.

Q)

WHAT KIND OF BALL DOESN'T BOUNCE?

A)

A SNOWBALL.

Q)

WHAT DID ONE SNOWMAN SAY ANOTHER SNOWMAN?

A)

YOU'RE COOL.

Q)

WHAT IS EVERY PARENT'S FAVORITE CHRISTMAS CAROL?

A)

SILENT NIGHT.

Q)

HOW DO CHICKENS DANCE AT A HOLIDAY PARTY?

A)

CHICK TO CHICK.

Q)

WHAT DO YOU GET WHEN SANTA PLAYS DETECTIVE?

A)

SANTA CLUES!

Q)

WHAT'S THE DIFFERENCE BETWEEN THE CHRISTMAS ALPHABET AND THE REGULAR ALPHABET?

A)

THE CHRISTMAS ALPHABET HAS NOEL.

Q)

WHAT FALLS BUT NEVER GETS HURT?

A)

SNOW.

Q)

WHAT KIND OF MUSIC DO ELVES LIKE?

A)

"WRAP" MUSIC.

Q)

HOW MUCH DID SANTA'S SLEIGH COST?

A)

NOTHING! IT WAS ON THE HOUSE.

Q)

WHAT DO YOU CALL A SNOWMAN WITH A SIX-PACK?

A)

THE ABDOMINAL SNOWMAN.

Q)

WHAT SNACK SHOULD YOU MAKE FOR THE SNOWMAN HOLIDAY PARTY?

A)

ICE KRISPY TREATS

Q)

WHAT DOES AN ELF WORK ON AFTER SCHOOL?

A)

HIS GNOMEWORK.

Q)

WHAT DO YOU CALL A SNOWMAN IN JULY?

A)

A PUDDLE.

Q)

WHY DID THE LITTLE BOY BRING HIS CHRISTMAS TREE TO THE HAIR SALON?

A)

IT NEED A LITTLE TRIM.

Q)

WHY DIDN'T THE TREE GET A PRESENT?

A)

HE WAS KNOTTY.

Q)

WHAT DOES SANTA USE TO KEEP HIS HOUSE SPARKLING CLEAN?

A)

COMET.

Q)

WHAT DO GROUCHY SHEEP SAY DURING THE HOLIDAYS?

A)

BAAAAAA HUMBUG!

Q)

WHAT DO YOU GET WHEN YOU CROSS AN IPHONE WITH A CHRISTMAS TREE?

A)

A PINE-APPLE!

Q)

WHAT DID ONE SNOWMAN SAY TO THE OTHER?

A)

DO YOU SMELL CARROTS?

Q)

HOW DO YOU HELP SOMEONE WHO HAS LOST THEIR CHRISTMAS SPIRIT?

A)

NURSE THEM BACK TO ELF.

Q)

WHAT DO SANTA'S ELVES DRIVE?

A)

MINIVANS.

Q)

WHAT IS A CHRISTMAS TREE'S FAVORITE CANDY?

A)

ORNA-MINTS!

Q)

WHAT DO YOU CALL A CAT SITTING ON THE BEACH ON CHRISTMAS EVE?

A)

SANDY CLAWS.

Q)

WHY DOES EVERYONE LOVE FROSTY THE SNOWMAN?

A)

HE'S COOL.

Q)

WHY DID THE CHRISTMAS TREE GO TO THE BARBER?

A)

IT NEEDED TO BE TRIMMED.

Q)

WHAT DO YOU CALL AN ELF WEARING EARMUFFS?

A)

ANYTHING YOU WANT—HE CAN'T HEAR YOU!

Q)

WHY DON'T ALIENS CELEBRATE CHRISTMAS?

A)

BECAUSE THEY DON'T WANT TO GIVE AWAY THEIR PRESENCE.

Q)

WHAT DO YOU CALL A GREEDY ELF?

A)

ELFISH.

Q)

WHAT DO REINDEER SAY BEFORE THEY TELL YOU A JOKE?

A)

THIS ONE'S GONNA SLEIGH YOU!

Q)

WHAT DOES AN ELF WORK ON AFTER SCHOOL?

A)

HIS GNOMEWORK.

Q)

WHY DID SANTA CLAUS GET A PARKING TICKET ON CHRISTMAS EVE?

A)

HE LEFT HIS SLEIGH IN A SNOW PARKING ZONE.

Q)

WHAT DO YOU CALL AN OLD SNOWMAN?

A)

WATER.

Q)

WHAT DO GINGERBREAD MEN USE WHEN THEY BREAK THEIR LEGS?

A)

CANDY CANES.

Q)

WHAT DOES SANTA USE TO KEEP HIS HOUSE SPARKLING CLEAN?

A)

COMET.

Q)

WHAT DID THE TEACHER SAY TO RUDOLPH WHEN HE DIDN'T PREPARE FOR HIS TEST ON THE CIVIL WAR?

A)

YOU'LL GO DOWN IN HISTORY!

Q)

HOW DOES THE SNOW GLOBE FEEL THIS YEAR?

A)

A LITTLE SHAKEN.

Q)

WHY ARE CHRISTMAS TREES SO BAD AT KNITTING?

A)

THEY DROP ALL THEIR NEEDLES.

Q)

WHO DELIVERS PRESENTS TO BABY SHARKS?

A)

SANTA JAWS.

Q)

WHAT'S RED, WHITE, AND BLUE AT CHRISTMAS?

A)

A SAD CANDY CANE.

Q)

WHAT DID THE JUDGE SAY TO THE ANGRY ADVENT CALENDAR?

A)

YOUR DAYS ARE NUMBERED!

Q)

WHAT KIND OF CHRISTMAS PRESENT JUST CAN'T BE BEAT?

A)

A BROKEN DRUM.

Q)

WHERE DOES SANTA GO WHEN CHRISTMAS IS OVER?

A)

ON VACATION TO A HO-HO-HO-TEL.

Q)

WHAT KIND OF CHRISTMAS CAROL DO YOU SING TO FRUIT?

A)

"WE WISH YOU A BERRY CHRISTMAS."

Q)

WHAT BODY PART DO YOU ONLY SEE AT CHRISTMAS?

A)

THE MISTLE-TOE.

Q)

HOW DO YOU KNOW WHEN SANTA'S AROUND?

A)

YOU CAN ALWAYS SENSE HIS PRESENTS.

Q)

WHAT DID THE STAMP SAY TO THE CHRISTMAS CARD?

A)

STICK WITH ME AND WE'LL GO PLACES.

Q)

WHAT DO YOU SING AT A SNOWMAN'S BIRTHDAY?

A)

"FREEZE A JOLLY GOOD FELLOW."

Q)

WHAT DO YOU CALL A SCARY LOOKING REINDEER?

A)

A CARI-BOO.

Q)

WHY DON'T YOU EVER SEE SANTA IN THE HOSPITAL?

A)

BECAUSE HE HAS PRIVATE ELF CARE!

Q)

WHY IS IT GETTING HARDER TO BUY ADVENT CALENDARS?

A)

THEIR DAYS ARE NUMBERED!

Q)

WHAT DO YOU CALL A BROKE SANTA?

A)

SAINT NICKEL-LESS

Q)

WHAT DID THE BEAVER SAY TO THE CHRISTMAS TREE?

A)

NICE GNAWING YOU!

Q)

WHY DON'T CRABS CELEBRATE CHRISTMAS?

A)

BECAUSE THEY'RE SHELL-FISH.

Q)

WHAT DOES THE GINGERBREAD MAN PUT ON HIS BED?

A)

COOKIE SHEETS!

Q)

HOW DOES A SHEEP SAY MERRY CHRISTMAS?

A)

FLEECE NAVIDAD!

Q)

IN WHAT YEAR DOES NEW YEAR'S DAY COME BEFORE CHRISTMAS?

A)

EVERY YEAR!

Q)

WHAT DOES AN ELF STUDY IN SCHOOL?

A)

THE ELF-ABET.

Q)

WHAT IS A BIRD'S FAVORITE CHRISTMAS STORY?

A)

THE FINCH WHO STOLE CHRISTMAS.

Q)

WHAT KIND OF MOTORCYCLE DOES SANTA LIKE TO RIDE?

A)

A HOLLY DAVIDSON!

Q)

WHAT IS AN ELF'S FAVORITE SPORT?

A)

NORTH-POLE VAULTING.

Q)

HOW DOES A SNOWMAN LOSE WEIGHT?

A)

HE WAITS FOR THE WEATHER TO GET WARMER!

Q)

WHAT DOES MRS. CLAUS SAY TO SANTA WHEN THERE ARE CLOUDS IN THE SKY?

A)

IT LOOKS LIKE RAIN, DEER.

Q)

WHO DELIVERS CHRISTMAS PRESENTS TO ELEPHANTS?

A)

ELEPHANTA CLAUS.

Q)

WHY DOES SANTA WORK AT THE NORTH POLE?

A)

BECAUSE THE PENGUINS KICKED HIM OUT OF THE SOUTH POLE!

Q)

WHY DIDN'T RUDOLPH GET A GOOD REPORT CARD?

A)

BECAUSE HE WENT DOWN IN HISTORY.

Q)

WHAT DOES JACK FROST LIKE BEST ABOUT SCHOOL?

A)

SNOW AND TELL.

Q)

WHAT KIND OF BALL DOESN'T BOUNCE?

A)

A SNOWBALL.

Q)

WHAT'S THE GRINCH'S LEAST FAVORITE BAND?

A)

THE WHO!

Q)

WHAT HAPPENED TO THE MAN WHO STOLE AN ADVENT CALENDAR?

A)

HE GOT 25 DAYS!

Q)

HOW DID THE ORNAMENT GET ADDICTED TO CHRISTMAS?

A)

HE WAS HOOKED ON TREES HIS WHOLE LIFE.

Q)

WHY WAS SANTA'S LITTLE HELPER DEPRESSED?

A)

BECAUSE HE HAD VERY LOW ELF ESTEEM.

Q)

WHAT DOES THE GRUNCH DO WITH A BASEBALL BAT?

A)

HITS A GNOME AND RUNS.

Q)

WHAT DO FISH SING DURING THE HOLIDAYS?

A)

CHRISTMAS CORALS.

Q)

WHAT IS A CHRISTMAS TREE'S FAVORITE CANDY?

A)

ORNAMINTS.

Q)

WHAT DID SANTA DO WHEN HE WENT SPEED DATING?

A)

HE PULLED A CRACKER!

Q)

WHAT DO YOU CALL A KID WHO DOESN'T BELIEVE IN SANTA?

A)

A REBEL WITHOUT A CLAUS.

Q)

WHERE DO POLAR BEARS VOTE?

A)

THE NORTH POLL!

Q)

WHY DID FROSTY ASK FOR A DIVORCE?

A)

HIS WIFE WAS A TOTAL FLAKE.

Q)

WHAT DO YOU GET IF YOU CROSS SANTA WITH A DUCK?

A)

A CHRISTMAS QUACKER!

Q)

WHY DOES SCROOGE LOVE REINDEER SO MUCH?

A)

BECAUSE EVERY SINGLE BUCK IS DEAR TO HIM!

Q)

WHAT GOES "OH, OH, OH"?

A)

SANTA WALKING BACKWARDS!

Q)

WHAT'S SANTA'S FAVORITE SNACK FOOD?

A)

CRISP PRINGLES.

Q)

WHY WAS THE SNOWMAN LOOKING THROUGH THE CARROTS?

A)

HE WAS PICKING HIS NOSE!

Q)

WHY DOES SANTA HAVE THREE GARDENS?

A)

SO HE CAN 'HO HO HO'!

Q)

HOW MUCH DID SANTA PAY FOR HIS SLEIGH?

A)

NOTHING. IT WAS ON THE HOUSE!

Q)

HOW DO YOU HELP SOMEONE WHO'S LOST THEIR CHRISTMAS SPIRIT?

A)

NURSE THEM BACK TO ELF.

Q)

WHAT DO SNOWMEN WEAR ON THEIR HEADS?

A)

ICE CAPS!

Q)

WHAT DID ADAM SAY THE DAY BEFORE CHRISTMAS?

A)

"IT'S CHRISTMAS, EVE!"

Q)

WHAT DO YOU CALL A BLIND REINDEER?

A)

I HAVE NO EYE DEER.

Q)

WHY DOES SANTA CLAUS GO DOWN THE CHIMNEY ON CHRISTMAS EVE?

A)

BECAUSE IT SOOT'S HIM.

Q)

WHAT'S THE DIFFERENCE BETWEEN SANTA AND A KNIGHT?

A)

ONE SLAYS THE DRAGON, THE OTHER DRAGS THE SLEIGH.

Q)

WHY DID THE CHRISTMAS TREE GO TO THE BARBER?

A)

IT NEEDED TO BE TRIMMED!

Q)

WHAT IS SANTA CLAUS' LAUNDRY DETERGENT OF CHOICE?

A)

YULE-TIDE.

Q)

HOW DOES SANTA KEEP HIS BATHROOM TILES IMMACULATE?

A)

HE USES COMET.

Q)

WHAT IS SANTA'S FAVORITE PIZZA?

A)

ONE THAT'S DEEP-PAN, CRISP AND EVEN!

Q)

WHAT DO THE ELVES CALL IT WHEN FATHER CHRISTMAS CLAPS HIS HANDS AT THE END OF A PLAY?

A)

SANTAPPLAUSE!

Q)

HOW WILL CHRISTMAS DINNER BE DIFFERENT AFTER BREXIT?

A)

NO BRUSSELS.

Q)

DID YOU KNOW THAT SANTA'S NOT ALLOWED TO GO DOWN CHIMNEYS THIS YEAR?

A)

IT WAS DECLARED UNSAFE BY THE ELF AND SAFETY COMMISSION.

Q)

WHY ARE COMET, CUPID, AND DONNER, AND ALWAYS WET?

A)

BECAUSE THEY ARE RAIN DEER.

Q)

WHEN SANTA IS ON THE BEACH WHAT DO THE ELVES CALL HIM?

A)

SANDY CLAUS

Q)

WHAT DO YOU GET IF SANTA GOES DOWN THE CHIMNEY WHEN A FIRE IS LIT?

A)

CRISP KRINGLE.

Q)

WHAT IS THE BEST EVIDENCE THAT MICROSOFT HAS A MONOPOLY?

A)

SANTA CLAUS HAD TO SWITCH FROM CHIMNEYS TO WINDOWS.

Q)

WHAT'S THE MOST POPULAR CHRISTMAS CAROL IN THE DESERT?

A)

OH CAAAMEL YE FAITHFUL.

Q)

WHAT'S AS BIG AS SANTA BUT WEIGHS NOTHING?

A)

SANTA'S SHADOW!

Q)

WHO IS NEVER HUNGRY AT CHRISTMAS?

A)

THE TURKEY—HE'S ALWAYS STUFFED!

Q)

WHAT IS THE MOST COMPETITIVE SEASON?

A)

WIN-TER!

Q)

WHY WOULDN'T THE CAT CLIMB THE CHRISTMAS TREE?

A)

IT WAS AFRAID OF THE BARK!

Q)

DID YOU KNOW SANTA CLAUS IS GOOD AT KARATE?

A)

IT'S TRUE, HE HAS A BLACK BELT!

Q)

WHO DELIVERS PRESENTS TO PETS?

A)

SANTA PAWS!

Q)

WHAT DO MONKEYS SING AT CHRISTMAS?

A)

JUNGLE BELLS!

Q)

WHAT DO YOU GET IF YOU CROSS A BELL WITH A SKUNK?

A)

JINGLE SMELLS!

Q)

HOW MANY PRESENTS CAN SANTA FIT IN HIS SACK FOR BAD CHILDREN?

A)

ZERO!

Q)

WHAT DID SANTA CLAUSE SAY TO WHEN HE CRASHED HIS SLEIGH?

A)

WELL, NOW I'M REALLY SCROOGED.

Q)

WHAT DO ELVES DO AFTER SCHOOL?

A)

THEIR GNOME WORK.

Q)

WHAT'S RED, WHITE AND BLUE AT CHRISTMAS TIME?

A)

A SAD CANDY CANE!

Q)

WHAT COMES AT THE END OF CHRISTMAS?

A)

THE LETTER "S"!

Q)

WHAT DO ANGRY MICE SEND TO EACH OTHER IN DECEMBER?

A)

CROSS MOUSE CARDS!

Q)

WHAT'S A SNOWMAN'S FAVORITE CEREAL?

A)

FROSTY FLAKES

Q)

WHY IS SANTA SO JOLLY?

A)

HE HAS A REALLY GREAT SENSE OF ELF.

Q)

WHERE DOES SANTA GO WHEN CHRISTMAS IS OVER?

A)

TO A HO-HO-HO-TEL

Q)

WHAT DO REINDEER HANG ON THEIR CHRISTMAS TREES?

A)

HORN-AMENTS.

Q)

WHAT KIND OF CHRISTMAS CAROLS DO YOU SING TO FRUIT?

A)

HAVE YOURSELF A BERRY LITTLE CHRISTMAS

Q)

WHAT DID RUDOLPH SAY ABOUT THE BIG BOOK OF NOSES?

A)

I ALREADY RED THAT ONE.

Q)

DID YOU HEAR ABOUT THE KID WHO WAS SCARED OF SANTA?

A)

HE WAS CLAUS-TROPHOBIC.

Q)

WHAT IS THE BEST CHRISTMAS SONG TO SING TO YOUR PET ROCK?

A)

ROCKING AROUND THE CHRISTMAS TREE

Q)

WHAT DO SNOWMEN LIKE TO DO AT THE WEEKEND?

A)

JUST CHILL OUT.

Q)

WHAT SHOULD YOU SING AT A SNOWMAN'S BIRTHDAY PARTY?

A)

FREEZE A JOLLY GOOD FELLOW.

Q)

WHICH BODY PART DO YOU ONLY SEE AT CHRISTMAS?

A)

THE MISTLE-TOE.

Q)

WHAT DID SANTA SAY WHEN A REINDEER SNUCK UP ON HIM AND STUCK A TOOTH IN HIS ARM?

A)

OH, SILENT BITE!

Q)

WHAT DO YOU CALL A SNOW MONSTER THAT HAS A SIX-PACK?

A)

THE ABDOMINAL SNOWMAN

Q)

WHAT'S THE WEATHER REPORT EVER CHRISTMAS EVE?

A)

THERE'S A 100 PERCENT CHANCE OF REINDEER.

Q)

WHAT'S FROSTY'S FAVORITE DESERT?

A)

ICE KRISPIE TREATS.

Q)

WHY DID THE GINGERBREAD MAN GO TO THE DOCTOR?

A)

BECAUSE HE WAS FEELING CRUMMY.

Q)

WHY WAS THE GINGERBREAD MAN ROBBED?

A)

BECAUSE OF HIS DOUGH.

Q)

WHY DO BASKETBALL PLAYERS LOVE GINGERBREAD COOKIES?

A)

WHY DO BASKETBALL PLAYERS LOVE GINGERBREAD COOKIES?

Q)

WHAT GAME DO REINDEER PLAY AT SLEEPOVERS?

A)

TRUTH-OR-DEER.

Q)

WHO WON HE RACE BETWEEN RUDOLPH AND PRANCER?

A)

RUDOLPH WON BY A NOSE!

Q)

HOW DO YOU GET INTO DONNER'S HOUSE?

A)

YOU RING THE "DEER"BELL.

Q)

WHAT DOES TARZAN SING AT CHRISTMAS?

A)

JUNGLE BELLS.

Q)

THIS YEAR EVEN THE TOYS ARE STRESSED OUT!

A)

YEAH, THEY CAME ALREADY WOUND UP.

Q)

WHO LIVES AT THE NORTH POLE, MAKES TOYS AND RIDES AROUND IN A PUMPKIN?

A)

CINDER-"ELF"-A.

Q)

WHAT'S SANTA'S FAVORITE SANDWICH?

A)

PEANUT BUTTER AND JOLLY.

Q)

WHY DID THE ELVES ASK THE TURKEY TO JOIN THE BAND?

A)

BECAUSE HE HAD THE DRUM STICKS.

Q)

WHY DID SANTA GET A TICKET ON CHRISTMAS EVE?

A)

HE LEFT HIS SLEIGH IN A SNOW PARKING ZONE.

Q)

WHAT DO YOU GET WHEN YOU CROSS A BELL WITH A SKUNK?

A)

JINGLE SMELLS.

CHRISTMAS KNOCK KNOCK JOKES

KNOCK. KNOCK.
Who's there?
HANNA.
Hanna who?
HANNA PARTRIDGE IN A PEAR TREE.

CHRISTMAS KNOCK KNOCK JOKES

KNOCK, KNOCK!
Who's there?
CHRIS.
Chris who?
CHRISTMAS IS HERE!

CHRISTMAS KNOCK KNOCK JOKES

KNOCK, KNOCK.
Who's there?
DEXTER.
Dexter, who?
DEXTER HALLS WITH
BOUGHS OF HOLLY.

CHRISTMAS KNOCK KNOCK JOKES

KNOCK, KNOCK.
Who's there?
DOUGHNUT.
Doughnut who?
DOUGHNUT OPEN GIFTS UNTIL CHRISTMAS DAY.

CHRISTMAS KNOCK KNOCK JOKES

KNOCK, KNOCK.
Who's there?
IMA.
Ima who?
IMA DREAMING OF A WHITE CHRISTMAS.

CHRISTMAS KNOCK KNOCK JOKES

KNOCK, KNOCK!
Who's there?
COAL.
Coal who?
COAL ME WHEN
SANTA'S ON HIS WAY.

CHRISTMAS KNOCK KNOCK JOKES

KNOCK, KNOCK!
Who's there?
OH, CHRIS.
Oh, Chris who?
OH CHRISTMAS TREE, OH CHRISTMAS TREE...

CHRISTMAS KNOCK KNOCK JOKES

KNOCK, KNOCK!
Who's there?
ELF.
Elf who?
ELF ME WRAP THIS PRESENT!

CHRISTMAS KNOCK KNOCK JOKES

KNOCK, KNOCK!
WHO'S THERE?
SNOW.
SNOW WHO?
SNOW TIME TO WASTE.
IT'S ALMOST CHRISTMAS!

CUTE CHRISTMAS RIDDLE

Q)

WHAT KIND OF CANDLE BURNS LONGER, A RED CANDLE OR A GREEN CANDLE?

A)

NEITHER, CANDLES ALWAYS BURN SHORTER!

Q)

IF A LION HAD A CHRISTMAS MUSIC ALBUM, WHAT WOULD IT BE CALLED?

A)

JINGLE SMELLS.

CUTE CHRISTMAS RIDDLE

Q)

WHO IS THE MOST IMPOLITE AND DISRESPECTFUL OF ALL THE REINDEER?

A)

RUDE-OLF

Q)

HOW MANY PRESENTS CAN SANTA FIT IN AN EMPTY SACK?

A)

ONLY ONE – AFTER THAT, IT'S NOT EMPTY ANYMORE!

CUTE CHRISTMAS RIDDLE

Q)

WHAT'S RED AND WHITE AND GOES UP AND DOWN AND UP AND DOWN?

A)

SANTA CLAUS STUCK IN AN ELEVATOR.

Q)

WHAT DO GRIZZLY BEARS DRAPE ON THEIR CHRISTMAS TREES?

A)

GRRR-LAND.

CUTE CHRISTMAS RIDDLE

Q)

WHAT HAS BARK BUT DOES NOT BITE?

A)

CHRISTMAS TREE.

Q)

WHAT DID THE CHRISTMAS TREE WEAR TO KEEP IT WARM?

A)

A FIR COAT.

CUTE CHRISTMAS RIDDLE

Q)

THERE IS A MAN THAT CAN NEVER ENJOY THE FIREPLACE, WHO IS THIS MAN?

A)

HE'S A SNOWMAN.

Q)

WHAT KIND OF EGG CAN YOU DRINK?

A)

EGGNOG.

CUTE CHRISTMAS RIDDLE

Q)

WHERE DOES CHRISTMAS COME BEFORE THANKSGIVING?

A)

IN THE DICTIONARY.

Q)

IT HAS TWO COLORS AND IS MINTY YET SWEET, EAT ONE AND YOU'LL BE "HOOKED"! WHAT IS IT?

A)

A CANDY CANE.

I HOPE YOU'VE ENJOYED THESE CHRISTMAS JOKES AND RIDDLES.

MERRY CHRISTMAS

Printed in Great Britain
by Amazon